WHAT TO DO WHEN Divorce IS THE ONLY OPTION?

An Alabama Divorce Lawyer's Guide to Effective Divorce and Child Custody Representation

Mitchell J. Howie, Esq.

Jacobs & Whitehall
9600 Escarpment Blvd
Suite 745-282
Austin, TX 78749
(888) 570-7338
www.jacobsandwhitehall.com

Ordering Information:

Quantity sales. Special discounts are available on quantity purchases by corporations, associations, and others. For details, contact the publisher at the address above.

Orders by U.S. trade bookstores and wholesalers. Please contact Jacobs & Whitehall: Tel: (888) 570-7338 or visit www.jacobsandwhitehall.com.

Printed in the United States of America

Published in 2024

ISBN: 978-1-954506-91-6

FOREWORD

I had wanted to write a book since I was a kid and was interested in sports and all books by Matt Christopher. Of course, I had imagined writing a novel, or a sports story, that would actively engage and entertain readers. While I have not gotten around to those sorts of books, this is my 3rd book in the legal field. My hope is that this informative book will provide crucial information for people going through what they likely view as one of their life's darkest moments.

What's more, I also hope this book will help guide individuals to the best representation they can get – in whatever state their divorce is occurring – so individuals and families can achieve the best possible outcome as they transition from one sort of family life to another. And hopefully this will help individuals come to view the divorce transition as the first step to an exciting next chapter rather than a purported *sad ending* or *failure* to a previous chapter in their lives.

DEDICATION

This third book is dedicated to my mom, Carol Howie, and my dad, Roger Schinella. I did not meet my dad until I was 32 years old. I sought my father out just a few months after my daughter was born. I am happy I got to meet him and learn about him and my Italian heritage before he passed away from cancer. My mom showed me how a single parent household must run and showed me the importance of relying on extended family to ensure a child knows the love and gets the support they need to learn and thrive. I would like to say, "***thanks mom!***" for all you did in serving the roles of my mom and dad! I use your model to give hope to single mothers going through a transition. I also use the "hole in my heart" from not having a father present (that you filled to the best of your ability) to advise dads on the importance of staying in their child's lives despite any relationship difficulties with their spouse. I love you both and thanks for all you (and your families did) to contribute to my life and happiness.

ACKNOWLEDGEMENTS

As always, I want to thank my wife Melanie, first and foremost for doing all of the *heavy lifting* at home to make our family work. Your daily labor of love in ensuring the kids have a safe, clean and comfortable environment to come home to; while ensuring our kids have completed their homework and studied; and making sure we have nutritious snacks and healthy meals throughout the day is never ending. The kids and I are eternally grateful to you for all your daily struggles to make our family life run so effectively. I know your experience running international computer programs all over the world before retiring from IBM is an invaluable asset to your program management of our lives and business! I often use your history of going through a previous divorce and being a single mother, as hope for all my family law clients on how a blended family can and should function for the best interests of the children involved. I also want to acknowledge all past and present clients for their faith in my firm for entrusting us with the huge responsibility and privilege of helping you and your family through a difficult time.

DISCLAIMER

This publication is intended to be used for educational purposes only. No legal advice is being given, and no Attorney-Client relationship is intended to be created by reading this material. The author assumes no liability for any errors or omissions or for how this book or its contents are used or interpreted, or for any consequences resulting directly or indirectly from the use of this book. For legal or any other advice, please consult an experienced attorney or the appropriate expert, who is aware of the specific facts of your case and is knowledgeable in the law in your jurisdiction.

Law Office of Mitchell J. Howie & Associates, P.L.L.C.

102 South Side Square

Huntsville, Alabama 35801

www.mitchellhowie.com

(256) 533-8074

TESTIMONIALS

"Huntsville child custody lawyer, Mitchell J. Howie is an outstanding lawyer and an exceptional human being. His knowledge of the law and great intellect make him a formidable Counselor. My case was unique, challenging, and spanned across multiple States. Mitchell's commitment to the rule of law and steadfast determination ensured we not only prevailed in Court but also won our cases on appeal creating new precedent for people who may be faced with similar legal hardships. I was unfamiliar with how to deal with the Courts, and it was Mitchell's guidance and support that enabled me to navigate through my difficult circumstances. Mitchell J. Howie is a principled man who strives for perfection and justice. It is because of his pure heart that he is able to passionately pursue his client's best interests. Mitchell really cares! I recommend him to anyone in need. I pray God keeps him well."

– Julie L.

****

"I strongly recommend Mitchell J. Howie as a Family Law attorney with the utmost integrity, intelligence,

knowledge of the law, sharp instincts, ability to understand the complexities of a case and stay focused on what is most important. He managed to get both parties to a settlement in less than a year in a very complex situation that involved legal issues in the US and abroad. Mitchell is personable, supportive and a pleasure to work with, as well. I would hire Mitchell again and recommend him highly.

— Jamon B.

****

"Absolutely top notch and outstanding legal counsel! The people at Mitchell J. Howie are the best Huntsville has to offer with regard to divorce law. He explained my options and worked to get a settlement that kept me out of court. Highly recommended!"

— M. Johnson

****

"I had never gotten divorced or been around anyone who was getting divorced enough to have a clue about where to start. Mr. Howie guided me through every step. He was patient as I started divorce proceedings then ended them a couple of times before I finally decided to go through with it for good. He gave me good advice about deciding which parts

of proposed agreements to accept and which to reject and helped me think through how to evaluate the financial aspects of changes in alimony and retirement accounts. I was able to get the divorce done almost entirely over email. If you have to get a divorce at all, I heartily recommend Mitchell J. Howie."

— Steve S.

****

"Best family attorney you can find! Mitchell and his team helped my family through an absolute nightmare. They were always there if I had questions, they always responded immediately, if Mitchell was in a meeting or on a call I was able to reach Madeline right away. They are compassionate, brilliant, and incredibly hard working. I would hire Mitchell 1,000 times over. I can't thank him enough.

— Carly W.

****

"Attorney Mitchell J. Howie is a professional and pleasant person to work with. In my dealings with him, he has been helpful, insightful and very accommodating to my needs and requests. I've been impressed with his consistent work ethic and his passion for helping those in need. Even in stressful situations, I have felt confident and at ease knowing that

Mitchell J. Howie is at the helm. If you want an advocate who is approachable and willing to stand by your side, I highly recommend Mr. Howie as your next attorney."

– Everett A.

****

"Mr. Howie and his paralegal team are truly the best! He is the kind of attorney that is meticulous, knowledgeable on child custody issues, detail oriented, and most of all takes the time to really understand your needs and your case. Mitch cares about having the best outcome for you and children. He is highly experienced working with divorces and also foreign services divorces. He got me my children back!!"

– Michael D.

****

"Huntsville Attorney Mitchell J. Howie is a warrior. He is relentless in his pursuit of justice for his client. Mitchell does not give up. My case was unprecedented, and Mitchell was up against the biggest law firm in town. I worried how one man could go up against all those sharks, but Mitchell was resilient. He showed no fear, and he stood up for me despite how difficult it was for him professionally. Mitchell is a man who does the right thing, even if it means he must put

everything on the line. He has integrity. Mitchell believes in equal application of the rule of law, regardless of financial or social status. Mitchell J. Howie is the type of lawyer that promotes justice. He has a deep desire to leave his clients in a better place. He does not just win a case; he fights for a cause. When he believes in something, he will prevail. We won an extraordinary victory in the Courts and were upheld on appeal numerous times. I am indebted to Mitchell for his great kindness and humanity. He is the type of human being that changes the world because of his pursuit for justice! I am proud to call him a friend.

– Maria L.

TABLE OF CONTENTS

About The Author

Since 2004 I've been a practicing attorney, initially opening my firm in Austin, Texas. However, the pull to serve in the military remained strong, an urge that began in my high school days when I contemplated going to the Naval Academy for my college experience.

This determination eventually led me to the JAG Corps after opening my legal practice – and I dedicated nearly five years of my life to active duty in the Air Force. I continue to serve in the reserves to this day, and I'm entrusted with the great responsibility of teaching trial advocacy to young JAGs across various military installations across the globe.

My first exposure to divorce as a lawyer emerged during my active-duty military service when I was serving as *Chief of Legal Assistance* at Davis Monthan Air Force base in Tucson, Arizona. This role had me interfacing with countless military personnel, explaining the fundamentals of divorce and its impact on both personal and professional fronts.

Upon my return to civilian life and the reopening of my civilian law practice, I felt compelled to continue assisting people through the divorce process because my upbringing in a single parent household led to a passion to help families and their children get through the divorce process. My passion has always been to serve, and through my legal practice, I continue to help clients and their families, guiding them through the legal landscape with utmost care and dedication. Because of my personal history and background, I am passionate about divorce and child custody legal work and continuing to serve those families that need legal assistance as they go through a difficult transition.

CHAPTER ONE

AN INTRODUCTION TO DIVORCE IN ALABAMA

Unfortunately, as with any other state across this great nation, divorce is common in Alabama. Of course, the reasons people divorce are complex and vary widely based on individual circumstances. However, some common factors that contribute to divorce often include:

- Communication challenges
- Infidelity

- Financial disagreements
- Financial Problems
- Diminished Intimacy
- Incompatibility
- Alcoholism
- Substance Misuse/Abuse
- Domestic Abuse
- Lack of Respect
- Parenting Differences
- Illnesses
- Deaths in Family
- Other Emotional Trauma
- Irreconcilable Differences

These factors, either in isolation or combined, can often steer relationships to a point of total breakdown. When this happens, divorce often feels like and becomes the only option to move forward.

Preparing For Divorce

No one ever said divorce was easy or uncomplicated. There are many layers, both emotional and financial, that you should prepare yourself for. In fact, there are several steps you can take even before either you, or your spouse, files a divorce that can put you in the best position possible when it comes to child custody**Error! Bookmark not defined.**, child support, and division of assets.

- Regardless of your circumstances, contacting a family law attorney should always be the top priority. Make sure you are consulting with a qualified family law attorney and divorce attorney who practices within the jurisdiction you plan to file in or where your spouse has filed. They can provide legal advice tailored to your situation and help you understand your rights and responsibilities.
- Gather your financial records. Collect any and all relevant information including passwords and logins to financial institutions. You'll also want to get copies of your tax returns, bank statements, property deeds, mortgage information, retirement account statements, and credit card statements. People sometimes find it surprising how little they actually know about their own finances until it is too late.

- Make a list of any assets and debts you and your spouse own that you are aware of – and remember to write down when each asset was acquired to include if it was acquired before or during the marriage. This inventory should include information about real estate, vehicles, valuable possessions, and any debts, like loans or credit card balances. This information will be useful when it comes time to identifying and dividing assets and debts in the likely upcoming divorce proceedings.
- Think about what will happen to your child (or children) during the divorce process and afterwards. Can you leave the marital home and take the children? Will you have financial support for yourself and your children while you wait for a divorce to be finalized? Consider your children's best interests and potential custody schedules that could work for both you and your spouse. Then, start getting prepared to discuss your realistic expectations with your attorney, or your spouse, as you move forward with the divorce process.

- Start setting yourself up for financial security. Before you file for divorce – or if you suspect your spouse is going to file – you should consider opening your own individual bank accounts or credit cards so that you have a safety net in place should you need it.

Divorce is often complicated and filing for divorce or waiting to be served can be a daunting next step. By having a well-thought-out plan in place, you will have a much easier transition into this next phase of your life.

The Process To File For A Divorce

To file for divorce in Alabama, you file your complaint and you allege the grounds for the divorce filing. These can either be based on an "irretrievable breakdown" or "incompatibility of temperament" (no-fault grounds) or attributing fault, like adultery, abuse, or cruelty. Alabama statutes list various permissible grounds for divorce. Once you, or your spouse has been served with the divorce papers, the person being served then has a 30-day window to reply.

Subsequently, you enter the discovery phase, which entails depositions, interrogatories, requests for production, requests for admissions, and various other informational gathering requests.

Where I practice, primarily in Huntsville, Alabama, a fully contested divorce typically has a trial date set not earlier than six months from the date of filing. More often, and in practice, the divorce trial is likely not held until 12 to 18 months after the filing. Once you appear before the judge for your divorce trial and the trial concludes, an order is issued regarding the legal issues in your case and then you finally receive a certificate of divorce along with your final divorce decree. At that point, you will be legally divorced from your spouse. That is the typical contested divorce route summary.

However, there is also the much quicker, easier, and inexpensive option of an uncontested divorce. This avenue is suitable if both parties can reach an agreement on all matters related to the divorce. To go uncontested, the parties must reach an agreement on the grounds of the divorce, and all matters including child custody, child visitation, child support, and the division of debts and assets, alimony, spousal support and other financial arrangements. If such an agreement, with all other necessary legal documents, is filed with the court through your attorneys, the expectation in Madison County is that the judge will issue an order to finalize your divorce within 30 days.

As you can see, uncontested divorces are much cheaper, much quicker, and much simpler. In fact, I often tell clients that the only clear winners in full-blown litigated divorce cases are the lawyers. However, it is important to remember that while an uncontested divorce might be impossible due to hurt feelings and raw emotions at the beginning of the divorce process, even a *contested divorce* can settle as an *uncontested divorce* at some point later in the process once "cooler heads prevail."

Where You File For Divorce

When deciding where to file for divorce, you have to look at the law and see if there's any benefit to filing in one state, or county, versus another. While this sometimes can be determined solely by the law and where the parties live, or where they are domiciled, certain circumstances can lead to a choice on where to file. This is an important consideration that you want an attorney to examine on the front end of the divorce process. For instance, North Carolina (at least during the time that I served there when I was on Active Duty) mandated a separation period of one year prior to commencing divorce proceedings. Understandably, few people wish to linger in a prolonged waiting period to file for divorce.

Alabama, on the other hand, doesn't impose any required separation period, allowing for divorce filings even while cohabitating with your spouse. Therefore, a divorce can be commenced in Alabama even when there is not a shared mutual understanding of separation with an intent to end the marriage. These are the kinds of considerations you want to have your divorce attorney look at before you file for divorce.

Factors That Might Impact A Divorce

In Alabama, being the spouse who files for divorce can have some impact on the divorce proceedings, but the extent of that impact will vary depending on the specific circumstances of the case.

For example, as the plaintiff (the person who files), you'll have control over when the process starts. This means you can take time to get prepared and only move forward when you are ready. As the plaintiff, you also will be establishing jurisdiction for the divorce proceedings as long as residency requirements are met. By filing first, you also have the opportunity to set the tone for the divorce by listing the grounds for which you are filing, and you can also outline your requests or concerns in that initial filing. Additionally, when you file first, you get to be the first to testify when testimony is taken before the Court.

From an emotional standpoint, being the spouse who initiates the divorce might offer a sense of control and empowerment for some, which can have psychological benefits during this challenging time. However, it is important to note that in Alabama, it doesn't really matter who files for divorce in the grand scheme of things and these factors might not significantly alter the outcome of the divorce itself.

Part of this is because, in Alabama, no one needs to prove fault or wrongdoing to obtain a divorce. Instead, the court's decisions on issues like property division, alimony, child custody, child visitation, and child support are generally based on factors such as the individual financial circumstances of the parties and the principles of equitable distribution, *best interests of the child standard,* and child support calculations pursuant to Alabama guidelines, rather than on who filed for divorce and the specific grounds.

A lot of people think that being the plaintiff in a family law case gives you an advantage because it means you're going to be able to testify before the judge before the other party has an opportunity to testify. Perhaps it's true that what comes out first "sticks in the judge's mind the best," but I don't know if I agree with that idea. It is just one consideration to take into account when deciding to initiate divorce proceedings.

Regardless of whether you're the spouse who files, or you are the spouse responding to the divorce filing, it's crucial to seek legal advice and counsel from an experienced divorce attorney to understand your rights and meet your legal responsibilities. Our firm can guide you through the legal proceedings, ensuring that your interests are protected and to help you try to achieve the best possible outcome for your situation.

CHAPTER TWO

CHILD CUSTODY, CHILD SUPPORT, ALIMONY, & THE DIVISION OF PROPERTY

When it comes to child custody decisions in Alabama, the guiding principle at play is for the Court to look at what is in the "best interests of the child." Courts comprehensively examine any factor of this kind that can help when making a custody determination, including but not limited to:

- Home Environment: This includes the physical location of the home, the quality of relationships between the parents and between each parent and the child, and daily responsibilities such as homework assistance, meal preparation, and discipline and the endless other aspects of parenting a child in a home.
- Parental Engagement: Courts evaluate the level of each parent's involvement in the child's life. A parent who has consistently been present and engaged is often viewed as the primary caretaker, influencing custody decisions. If one parent has often been absent due to work commitments, or other reasons, the court might lean towards the more present parent regarding custody decisions.
- Mental Health and Stability: The emotional and psychological well-being of the parents plays a crucial role in determining custody.
- Expert Opinions: In cases where abuse allegations arise, or alienation concerns are raised, the court

might rely on expert testimony to make informed decisions.

The Role Of A Child's Opinion

Most judges agree (and Alabama law holds) that the preference of a child younger than 12 years old is typically not going to be taken into account in a custody case.

Of course, based on individual circumstances, a judge can decide to listen to what a child has to say – and if a child is talking about abuse, their input is going to be considered. However, as far as a child "wanting" to go with mom or dad, the judge may give that preference some consideration, but it will typically not be a deciding factor.

Even for older children, although their opinions might be taken into account, the emphasis from the Court depends heavily on the child's maturity and other individual circumstances that are highly factually dependent. It is generally unlikely for courts to solely rely on a teenager's *preference* without weighing a host of other crucial factors.

Options If You Travel A Lot For Work

Travel demands of a job can significantly impact parenting plans. If one parent, be it Dad or Mom, is primarily homebound and acting as the main caregiver, a court may lean towards awarding them sole physical custody, given that they are the one at home raising the child.

On the other hand, if you travelled a lot previously but can show that you are not traveling for the next three or four years and your kids are teenagers, you could have an opportunity to convince the Judge for you to have the children just as much as your spouse.

The good news here is that there are numerous options for parenting plans that can be individually designed to meet any divorcing couple's circumstances. For example, I've seen custody plans where one parent has to travel a lot for work, so an agreement is made that when that parent is home, they're going to have an extensive amount of time with the child. In the end, it really depends on everyone's individual family situation and the ability of the parents to come to an agreement and be flexible with one another. The overarching goal is for everyone to hopefully work towards an agreement that promotes the best interests of the children involved.

Child Support Guidelines

Child support will always vary depending on the individual circumstances of a case. Generally speaking, child support is going to be determined using Alabama Child Support Guidelines pursuant to Rule 32 of the Alabama Rules of Judicial Administration. This framework provides a formula to establish the basic child support obligation based on the combined gross incomes of both parents, any monthly *"health care premiums"* paid by either parent, and any monthly *"necessary work-related child-care expenses"* and the number of children involved.

These guidelines can also take into account a number of other factors to ensure that the child's financial needs are met while considering both parents' financial circumstances. These factors can include:

- Each parent's gross income, including wages, salaries, self-employment income, bonuses, etc.
- The amount of time the child spends with each parent.
- Child support obligations for other children from a previous relationship.
- The presence of a child with special needs.
- Travel expenses necessary to achieve meaningful visitation.
- And more.

I have included the child support forms that are used to establish child support obligations in Alabama in the appendix of this book. Hopefully these forms will help folks better understand the calculations for basic child support in accordance with Rule 32.

In addition to the basic child support obligation, both parents may be held, or agree to be responsible for sharing additional child-related expenses such as health insurance, medical costs, daycare expenses, and educational expenses. These expenses can be divided based on the percentage of each parent's income in a pro rata fashion by agreement of the parties, or by order of the Court.

Overall, while these guidelines provide an outline for child support calculations, the final outcome is going to be determined by the specifics of each family's circumstance. Regardless of whether you are the spouse who files for divorce, or you are the spouse responding to the divorce filing, our firm can guide you through the legal proceedings, ensuring that your interests are protected and that you achieve the best possible outcome for your situation and your children.

Custody Or Child Support Order Modifications

In Alabama, child custody and child support can be modified if there is a material change in circumstance affecting the child's welfare. A "material change" could include developments such as a parent's relocation, remarriage, or the welfare of the child being at risk, among other factors. In some cases, a change in custody in Alabama could be modified based on the changing needs or preferences of the child, as well.

When it comes to child support, a "material change" could be triggered under Alabama law due to a substantial change in a parent's income or the relocation of a parent, which may lead to additional travel costs and less parenting time. Anything that has changed a parent's income or a parent's ability to contribute to a child's financial needs may be considered when it comes to a request to change child support orders.

Another consideration you want your child custody lawyer to understand and explain is how and when the "*McLendon Burden*" comes into effect after a parent has been given *sole physical custody* through a settlement agreement in a custody order and/or by a contested custody order. The *McLendon Burden* is set out in Alabama case law. See *Ex Parte McLendon*, 455 So.2d 863 (Ala. 1984). Invoking the *McLendon Burden/Standard* basically means a party faces a much steeper challenge (than the "best interest of the child standard") to demonstrate that a court should order a custody change. Our firm typically advises that the parent who receives "sole physical custody will be on the *McLendon Mountaintop* to rhetorically demonstrate that the other parent is going to have a very steep burden to overcome in proving that a change in custody is warranted. The *McLendon Burden* requires the party seeking a change in custody to show "substantially changed circumstances" and prove that the requested change will materially promote the best interest and welfare of the child. The *McLendon Burden* further requires that those "material benefits" be proven to offset the *inherent disruptive effects* to the child's stability and regular routine resulting from a change in custody. Because of this severe burden shift established after a party receives sole physical custody, it is critically important to ensure you understand this framework when handling child custody decisions that could impact the entirety of your child's life.

Alimony Or Spousal Support

Alimony or spousal support isn't a guaranteed outcome in divorces and is based on a multitude of factors as outlined in Alabama Statutes and Alabama Case law. Alabama Code Section 30-2-57 lists voluminous factors for the Court to consider in determining if and when alimony should be awarded. It specifically lists factors concerning the "ability to pay" of the payor and the "needs" of the payee. Further there are specific statutory factors for the Court to consider in determining whether it is equitable for the Court to award rehabilitative or periodic alimony. Specifically, Alabama Code Section 30-2-57(f) stipulates that the Court shall consider all relevant factors including all of the following:

(1) The length of the marriage.

(2) The standard of living to which the parties became accustomed during the marriage.

(3) The relative fault of the parties for the breakdown of the marriage.

(4) The age and health of the parties.

(5) The future employment prospects of the parties.

(6) The contribution of the one party to the education or earning ability of the other party.

(7) The extent to which one party reduced his or her income or career opportunities for the benefit of the other party or the family.

(8) Excessive or abnormal expenditures, destruction, concealment, or fraudulent disposition of property.

(9) All actual damages and judgments from conduct resulting in criminal conviction of either spouse in which the other spouse or child of the marriage was the victim.

(10) Any other factor the court deems equitable under the circumstances of the case.

Your divorce lawyer will be able to explain these factors to you and how they could be argued or perceived by the Court.

Typically, there are three main types of alimony recognized in Alabama to include: 1) *Pendente Lite Alimony* (spousal support occurring during the pendency of the divorce), 2) *Rehabilitative Alimony* which is limited to 5 years in duration absent extraordinary expenses pursuant to Alabama Code 30-2-57(b); and 3) *Periodic/Permanent Alimony.* What's more, the law in Alabama provides that the duration of periodic alimony cannot typically exceed the length of the marriage. For instance, if a marriage spanned 10 years, alimony can be granted for a maximum of those

10 years. Generally, only once a marriage has lasted for 20 years can the judge consider ordering "permanent alimony. See Alabama Code Section 30-2-57(g).

As one can see by reading Alabama law, alimony is based on many factors established in the individual marriage. However, the basic factors to be considered for an alimony award are the incomes of each party, the length of the marriage, the fault of the parties in contributing to the breakdown of the marriage, the health of the parties, the standard of living during the marriage, the ability of each party to earn, the ability to pay of the payor, and the demonstrated needs of the party receiving alimony.

Your attorney can give you a good idea as to whether or not alimony will be considered in your case, but in the end, the length of the marriage and the income of the parties are likely the most important threshold factors in determining whether any alimony will be considered and/or ordered.

Dividing Assets And Debts In A Divorce

In Alabama, the division of assets and debts during a divorce follows the principle of equitable distribution. This approach aims for a distribution that is fair and just, with consideration given to various factors, such as:

- **Marital Property v. Separate Property:** A key distinction is made between assets and debts acquired before the marriage and those acquired during the marriage. Typically, assets and debts amassed during the marriage are viewed as part of the marital assets subject to equitable distribution, while those acquired before the marriage can be considered separate property so long as the assets were not "commingled" under the law.
- **Asset & Debt Valuation:** The value of marital assets and debts will need to be determined. This includes tangible assets like real estate, jewelry, clothing, vehicles, retirement accounts, and bank accounts, as well as intangible assets like intellectual property, trademarks, pensions,

business valuations, or undefined retirement accounts. Simultaneously, debts such as mortgages, credit cards, car loans, personal loans can be taken into account and divided equitably.

- **Retirement and 401k Account Division:** Dividing Retirement Accounts can be particularly complex and require a Qualified Domestic Relations Order (QDRO), or a Retirement Benefits Court Order (RBCO).
- **Additional Considerations:** The court evaluates a number of other factors, including the duration of the marriage, monetary and non-monetary contributions made by each spouse to the marital estate, and the individual needs and circumstances of each party, among other things.

It's important to note that equitable distribution does not always mean equal distribution. The law requires the court to consider all of these factors when deciding how to divide assets and debts equitably in order to achieve a division that is fair given the unique circumstances of each case.

Resolving Asset And Debt Division Issues In A Divorce

In your pleadings, you can specify that there was separate property, such as an inheritance. If that separate property was not "comingled", then your position with the judge is that "separate asset" is not subject to equitable division by the divorce court. Separate property is an issue that you may deal with in Alabama Divorce proceedings. However, if separate property has been "comingled" (generally meaning that the asset has been used regularly for the benefit of the married couple) then the asset will be subject to equitable division.

Chapter Three

Finalizing & Modifying Divorce

Modifying A Final Divorce Decree

In Alabama, certain components of a final divorce decree can be altered if there's a substantial material change in circumstances. Generally, modifiable sections encompass child custody, child support, and spousal support. However, divisions of property finalized in the decree are not eligible for modification as property settlements are "non-modifiable" under Alabama law.

Examples of a substantial and material change in circumstances to modify aspects of a divorce order may include:

- Changes in employment status or significant salary fluctuations.
- Incarceration of a parent and/or the development of alcoholism or substance addiction issues.
- Relocating children nearer or farther from the other parent, potentially leading to a desire for increased physical custody and/or altering the visitation schedule. (The Alabama Parent Child Relationship Protection Act is invoked for any relocations.)

To avoid having to go back to court multiple times, it's a good idea to try to anticipate any of these foreseeable changes and, if permitted by the court, integrate provisions addressing any expected changes by agreement directly in your original divorce decree.

Finalizing Divorce

Assuming a case is settled by agreement, the parties will submit their agreement and a Final Decree of divorce to the court for final review. This settlement agreement and decree outlines all the settled terms, covering all areas of the marital dissolution to include the grounds for divorce, property division, alimony, child support, child custody, child visitation, and other important matters. If the court finds the terms fair and in compliance with Alabama law, the decree is signed by the judge and becomes legally binding.

Something to keep in mind is that, while it may be preferable, not all matters in a divorce can be settled before the divorce trial is held in Alabama. The parties can submit stipulations and/or a partial agreement on the areas where they agree and then litigate the remaining issues the parties simply cannot agree on. If that occurs, after a trial, the Court will grant the petition for divorce and accept the agreement as to the partial settlement and then issue an order establishing custody, child support, visitation, spousal support and all other matters that were not fully resolved prior to the trial.

All in all, it's important to remember that each divorce case is unique, and the timeline and process can vary based on your individual circumstances. So, if you are looking to navigate the divorce process smoothly and ensure that your rights are protected, you should not go through the process alone. Consider hiring an experienced family law attorney who can guide you through the specific requirements of finalizing a divorce in Alabama (or whatever state you are located) and make sure that your best interests, your children's best interests, and ultimately your family's best interests are championed at each step of the way.

CHAPTER FOUR

WHY HIRE AN EXPERIENCED DIVORCE LAWYER?

Going through a divorce can be one of the most challenging times in anyone's life. The feelings of loss, guilt, failure, embarrassment, fear of the future, and uncertainty can lead many to make emotional and not well reasoned decisions. Furthermore, considering the fact that "property settlements" under Alabama law are non-modifiable, and that the initial "child custody determination" by an Alabama court sometimes invokes the "*McLendon Burden*" it is absolutely imperative that you seek out an experienced divorce and child custody lawyer to protect your financial interests and the wellbeing of your children.

Trying to handle your divorce with an inexperienced divorce lawyer (*or even worse, on your own*) is likely not a sound decision when you consider the profound issues that are being decided. This is especially true when you consider the fact that your emotions may be clouding your generally good sense of reason and logic.

It is important to remember that the decisions made in your initial divorce and child custody case can have a lasting and permanent impact on the rest of your life. Accordingly, it is necessary to ensure you have the right legal representation to ensure you protect your legal rights and your children's best interests. With the right legal representation, hopefully you can prepare to ensure the next chapter of your life is the best. With a skilled divorce lawyer, hopefully you will be able to move efficiently forward through the divorce and then ultimately transition from the divorce process to your *new family life.*

What Is The Next Step?

The Law Office of Mitchell J. Howie & Associates, P.L.L.C. is a full-service firm providing expert counsel and services in divorce, child custody, child support, spousal support, division of assets, establishing paternity, child custody modifications, and all other areas of family law in Alabama. For a strategic legal consultation on any divorce, or Family Law related issue in Alabama, you can visit us at www.mitchellhowie.com, or e mail us at info@mitchellhowie.com, or call us today at 256-533-8074.

APPENDIX

a. Child Support Form 41

State of Alabama
Unified Judicial System
Form CS-41 Rev. 7/2019

CHILD-SUPPORT-OBLIGATION INCOME STATEMENT/AFFIDAVIT

Case Number

IN THE ______________ **COURT OF** ______________ **COUNTY, ALABAMA**
(Circuit or District) (Name of County)

Plaintiff ______________ **v. Defendant** ______________

AFFIDAVIT

I, ______________, being duly sworn upon my oath, state as follows :
(Name of Affiant)

1. I am the ☐ Plaintiff ☐ Defendant ☐ Other (please specify): ______________ in the above matter.
   My Social Security number is: XXX-XX-X______ LAST THREE (3) DIGITS ONLY
2. I am ☐ currently employed. My employer's name and address are:
   ____
   ____

   ☐ not currently employed.
   My last employer's name and address are: ______________
   ____
   Last position title: ______________
   Average monthly salary in the last year of employment: $
3. My monthly gross income includes:
   (For example of income that must be included, see back of this form. If income varies by month, enter the estimated average monthly gross income.)

Employment income	$______________
Self-employment income	$______________
Other employment-related income	$______________
Other non-employment-related income	$______________
Total	$______________

4. I incur the following amount monthly for work-related child-care: $______________ *(if none, write "None")*
5. The child(ren) of the parties is/are
   ☐ not covered by health-care coverage from me and/or my employer. ☐ Health-care coverage is available at a cost of $______ per month.
   ☐ covered by Medicaid or other public health-care coverage at no cost to me.
   ☐ covered by health-care coverage, and (1) I pay $______ each month, or that amount is paid on my behalf each month by my ______, for the family policy coverage under which the child(ren) is/are covered; and (2) the total number of persons covered under that policy is ______________.
   The pro rata portion of the health-care coverage cost attributable to the child or children who are the subject of the support order (which shall be calculated by dividing the total health-care coverage cost actually paid by, or on behalf of, the parent ordered to provide the coverage by the total number of persons (adult and/or children) covered and then multiplying the result by the number of children who are the subject of the support order) is the sum of $______________ .
   The health-care-coverage company's name and address are: ______________
   ______________.
6. I pay the following total amount for ☐ child support ☐ alimony in [a] prior case(s) as follows:
   [List case number(s) and county(ies) and state(s) here]:
   ______________ $______________
   (if none, write "None")
   ____

I understand that I will be required to maintain all income documentation used in preparing this Income Statement/Affidavit *(including my most recent income-tax return)* and that such documentation shall be made available as directed by the court. I also understand that any intentional falsification of the information presented in this Income Statement/Affidavit may subject me to the penalties of perjury.

____
Affiant

Sworn to and subscribed before me this ______ day of ______________, ________

____
Notary/Clerk

Form CS-41 (Back) Rev. 7/2019

EXAMPLES OF INCOME THAT MUST BE INCLUDED IN YOUR GROSS MONTHLY INCOME

1. Employment Income – shall include, but not be limited to, salary, wages, bonuses, commissions, severance pay, worker's compensation, pension income, unemployment insurance, disability insurance, and Social Security benefits.

2. Self-Employment Income – shall include, but not be limited to, income from self-employment, rent, royalties, proprietorship of a business, or joint ownership of a partnership or closely held corporation. "Gross income" means gross receipts minus ordinary and necessary expenses required to produce this income.

3. Other Employment-Related Income – shall include, but not be limited to, the average monthly value of any expense reimbursements or in-kind payments received in the course of employment that are significant and reduce personal living expenses, such as a furnished automobile, a clothing allowance, and a housing allowance.

4. Other Non-Employment-Related Income – shall include, but not be limited to, dividends, interest, annuities, capital gains, gifts, prizes, and preexisting periodic alimony.

RULE 32, ALABAMA RULES OF JUDICIAL ADMINISTRATION, PROVIDES THE FOLLOWING DEFINITIONS:

Income. For purposes of the guidelines specified in this Rule, "income" means the actual gross income of a parent, if the parent is employed to full capacity, or if the parent is unemployed or underemployed, then it means the actual gross income the parent has the ability to earn.

Gross Income.

"Gross income" includes income from any source, and includes, but is not limited to, income from salaries, wages, commissions, bonuses, dividends, severance pay, pensions, interest, trust income, annuities, capital gains, Social Security benefits, Veteran's benefits, workers' compensation benefits, unemployment-insurance benefits, disability-insurance benefits, gifts, prizes, and preexisting periodic alimony.

"Gross income" does not include child support received for other children or benefits received from means-tested public-assistance programs, including, but not limited to, Temporary Assistance for Needy Families, Supplemental Security Income, food stamps, and general assistance.

Self-employment Income.

For income from self-employment, rent, royalties, proprietorship of business, or joint ownership of a partnership or closely held corporation, "gross income" means gross receipts minus ordinary and necessary expenses required to produce such income, as allowed by the Internal Revenue Service, with the exceptions noted in Rule 32 (B)(3)(b).

Under those exceptions, "ordinary and necessary expenses" does not include amounts allowable by the Internal Revenue Service for the accelerated component of depreciation expenses, investment tax credits, or any other business expenses determined by the court to be inappropriate for determining gross income for purposes of calculating child support.

Other Income. Expense reimbursements or in-kind payments received by a parent in the course of employment of self-employment or operation of a business shall be counted as income if they are significant and reduce personal living expenses.

b. Child Support Form 42 Revised July 2019

State of Alabama Unified Judicial System Form CS-42 Rev. 7/2019	CHILD-SUPPORT GUIDELINES	Case Number

IN THE ______________ (Circuit or District) COURT OF ______________ (Name of County) COUNTY, ALABAMA

______________ Plaintiff v. ______________ Defendant

Children	Date of Birth	Children	Date of Birth

	Plaintiff	Defendant	Combined
1. MONTHLY GROSS INCOME	$	$	
a. Minus Preexisting Child-Support Payment	-	-	
b. Minus Preexisting Periodic-Alimony Payment	-	-	
2. MONTHLY ADJUSTED GROSS INCOME	$	$	$
3. PERCENTAGE SHARE OF INCOME (Each parent's income on Line 2 divided by the Combined Income)	%	%	
4. BASIC CHILD-SUPPORT OBLIGATION (Apply Line 2 Combined to "Schedule of Basic Child-Support Obligations" (Appendix to Rule 32))			$
5. WORK-RELATED CHILD-CARE COSTS			+
6. HEALTH-CARE-COVERAGE COSTS			+
7. TOTAL CHILD-SUPPORT OBLIGATION (Add lines 4, 5, and 6)			$
8. EACH PARENT'S CHILD-SUPPORT OBLIGATION (Multiply Line 7 by Line 3)	$	$	
9. ADJUSTMENT FOR PAYMENT OF HEALTH-CARE COVERAGE (If obligor pays health-care coverage, enter amount in Line 6 in obligor's column)	-	-	
10. RECOMMENDED CHILD-SUPPORT ORDER (Subtract Line 9 from the amount on Line 8. Leave custodial parent's column blank.)	$	$	

Comments, Calculations, or Rebuttals to Guidelines:

PREPARED BY:	DATE:

c. Child Support Form 42 Revised May 2022

State of Alabama Unified Judicial System Form CS-42 Rev. 5/2022	CHILD SUPPORT GUIDELINES	Case Number

IN THE ______________________ COURT OF ______________________ COUNTY, ALABAMA

(Circuit or District) (Name of County)

______________________ v. ______________________

Plaintiff Defendant

Children	Date of Birth	Children	Date of Birth

Line	Item	Plaintiff	Defendant	Combined
		Number of Children		
1	MONTHLY GROSS INCOME	$	$	$
1a	Minus Preexisting Child-Support Payments	–	–	–
1b	Minus Preexisting Periodic Alimony Payments	–	–	–
2	MONTHLY ADJUSTED GROSS INCOME (Line 1 – Line 1a – Line 1b)	$	$	$
3	PERCENTAGE SHARE OF INCOME (Income on Line 2 divided by Combined Income)	%	%	100%
4	BASIC CHILD SUPPORT OBLIGATION (Apply Line 2 Combined to Schedule of Basic Child Support Obligations)			$
5	WORK-RELATED CHILD-CARE COSTS (Paid by Either Parent)	$	$	+
6	HEALTH-CARE-COVERAGE COSTS (Paid by Either Parent)	$	$	+
7	TOTAL CHILD-SUPPORT OBLIGATION (Combined Line 4 + Line 5 + Line 6)			$
8	EACH PARENT'S CHILD SUPPORT OBLIGATION (Line 3 x Line 7)	$	$	
9	TOTAL COSTS PAID BY EACH PARENT (Line 5 + Line 6)	–	–	
10	EACH PARENT'S ADJUSTED CHILD-SUPPORT OBLIGATION (Line 8 – Line 9. If less than $0, enter $0.)	$	$	
	Self-Support Reserve (SSR)			
11	INCOME AVAILABLE AFTER SSR (Line 2 – SSR of $981. If less than $0, enter $0.)	$	$	
12	INCOME AVAILABLE FOR SUPPORT (85% of Line 11. If less than $50, enter $50 minimum obligation.)	$	$	
	Recommended Child Support Order			
13	RECOMMENDED CHILD SUPPORT ORDER (Lesser of Lines 10 and 12)	$	$	

Comments, Calculations, or Rebuttals to Guidelines:

Prepared By: Date:

d. Child Support Form 42-S Revised June 2023

State of Alabama Unified Judicial System Form CS-42-S Effective 6/2023	CHILD SUPPORT GUIDELINES	Case Number

IN THE____________________COURT OF____________________COUNTY, ALABAMA
(Circuit or District) (Name of County)

______________________________v.______________________________
Plaintiff Defendant

Children	Date of Birth	Children	Date of Birth

Line	Item	Plaintiff	Defendant	Combined
		Number of Children		
1	MONTHLY GROSS INCOME	$	$	$
1a	Minus Preexisting Child-Support Payments	–	–	–
1b	Minus Preexisting Periodic Alimony Payments	–	–	–
2	MONTHLY ADJUSTED GROSS INCOME (Line 1 – Line 1a – Line 1b)	$	$	$
	Child-Support-Obligation Calculations	%	%	100 %
3	PERCENTAGE SHARE OF INCOME (Income on Line 2 divided by Combined Income)			
4	BASIC CHILD-SUPPORT OBLIGATION (Apply Line 2 Combined to Schedule of Basic Child-Support Obligations)			$
5	SHARED 50% PHYSICAL-CUSTODY CHILD-SUPPORT OBLIGATION (150% of Basic Child-Support Obligation) (1.5 x Line 4 Combined)			$
6	WORK-RELATED CHILD-CARE COSTS (Paid by Either Parent)	$	$	
7	HEALTH-CARE-COVERAGE COSTS (Paid by Either Parent)	+	+	
8	TOTAL CHILD-CARE AND HEALTH-CARE-COVERAGE COSTS (Line 6 + Line 7)	$	$	$
9	TOTAL CHILD-SUPPORT OBLIGATION (Combined Line 5 + Line 8)			$
10	EACH PARENT'S CHILD-SUPPORT OBLIGATION (Line 3 x Line 9)	$	$	
	Shared 50% Physical Custody Calculations			
11	TOTAL COSTS PAID BY EACH PARENT (Line 8)	–	–	
12	CREDIT FOR SHARED 50% PHYSICAL CUSTODY (50% of Line 5 Combined)	–	–	
13	ADJUSTED SHARED 50% PHYSICAL-CUSTODY CHILD-SUPPORT OBLIGATION (Line 10 – Line 11 – Line 12)	$	$	
	Recommended Child-Support Order			
14	RECOMMENDED CHILD-SUPPORT ORDER (Higher of amounts in Line 13 placed in column of parent with higher amount.)	$	$	

Comments, Calculations, or Rebuttals to Guidelines:

Prepared By: Date:

e. Child Support Form 43

State of Alabama Unified Judicial System Form CS-43 Rev. 7/2019	**CHILD-SUPPORT GUIDELINES NOTICE OF COMPLIANCE**	Case Number

IN THE ____________________ **COURT OF** ____________________ **COUNTY, ALABAMA**
(Circuit or District) (Name of County)

____________________ v. ____________________
Plaintiff Defendant

☐ Based upon the income and expenditures supplied by parties in Form CS-41, "Child-Support Obligation Income Statement/Affidavit," the child-support guidelines, as set out in Rule 32, Alabama Rules of Judicial Administration, have been followed and applied.

☐ The child-support guidelines, as set out in Rule 32, Alabama Rules of Judicial Administration, have not been followed and applied as they would be unjust or inappropriate because of the following reasons:

____
____
____
____.

The amount of support required under the child support guidelines would be $ ____________.

Date: ____________________ Date: ____________________

____________________ ____________________
Signature of Plaintiff Signature of Defendant

Signature of Plaintiff's Attorney Signature of Defendant's Attorney

____________________ ____________________
____________________ ____________________
Address of Plaintiff or Plaintiff's Attorney Address of Defendant or Defendant's Attorney

____________________ ____________________
Telephone No. of Plaintiff or Plaintiff's Attorney Telephone No. of Defendant or Defendant's Attorney

f. Income Withholding Order for Support

OMB 0970-0154
Expiration Date: 09/30/2023

INCOME WITHHOLDING FOR SUPPORT

I. Sender Information: (Completed by the Sender) **Date:** ____________

☐ **INCOME WITHHOLDING ORDER/NOTICE FOR SUPPORT** ☐ **AMENDED IWO**

☐ **(IWO) ONE-TIME ORDER/NOTICE FOR LUMP SUM PAYMENT** ☐ **TERMINATION OF IWO**

☐ Child Support Enforcement (CSE) Agency ☐ Court ☐ Attorney ☐ Private Individual/Entity (Check One)

NOTE: This IWO must be regular on its face. Under certain circumstances you must reject this IWO and return it to the sender (see IWO instructions www.acf.hhs.gov/css/resource/income-withholding-for-support-instructions). If you receive this document from someone other than a state or tribal CSE agency or a court, a copy of the underlying support order must be attached.

State/Tribe/Territory ALABAMA
City/County/Dist./Tribe ____________
Private Individual Entity ____________

Remittance ID (include w/payment) ____________
Order ID ____________
Case ID ____________

II. Employer and Case Information: (Completed by the Sender)

____
Employer/Income Withholder's Name
____
Employer/Income Withholder's Address
____
____

RE: ____________
Employee/Obligor's Name (Last, First, Middle)
____
Employee/Obligor's Social Security Number
____
Employee/Obligor's Date of Birth
____
Custodial Party/Obligee's Name (Last, First, Middle)

Employer/Income Withholder's FEIN ____________

Child(ren)'s Name(s) (Last, First, Middle)	Child(ren)'s Birth Date(s)

III. Order Information: (Completed by the Sender)

This document is based on the support order from ____________ (State/Tribe).
You are required by law to deduct these amounts from the employee/obligor's income until further notice.

$____________ Per ____________ current child support
$____________ Per ____________ past-due child support - Arrears greater than 12 weeks? ☐ Yes ☐ No
$____________ Per ____________ current cash medical support
$____________ Per ____________ past-due cash medical support
$____________ Per ____________ current spousal support
$____________ Per ____________ past-due spousal support
$____________ Per ____________ other (must specify) ____________

for a **Total Amount to Withhold** of **$** ________ per ____________.

IV. Amounts to Withhold: (Completed by the Sender)

You do not have to vary your pay cycle to be in compliance with the *Order Information*. If your pay cycle does not match the ordered payment cycle, withhold one of the following amounts:

$ ________ per weekly pay period
$ ________ per semimonthly pay period (twice a month)
$ ________ per biweekly pay period (every two weeks)
$ ________ per monthly pay period
$ ________ **Lump Sum Payment:** Do not stop any existing IWO unless you receive a termination order.

PAPERWORK REDUCTION ACT OF 1995 (Pub. L. 104-13) STATEMENT OF PUBLIC BURDEN: The purpose of this information collection is to provide uniformity and standardization. Public reporting burden for this collection of information is estimated to average two to five minutes per response, including the time for reviewing instructions, gathering and maintaining the data needed, and reviewing the collection of information. This is a mandatory collection of information in accordance with 45 CFR 303.100 of the Child Support Enforcement Program. An agency may not conduct or sponsor, and a person is not required to respond to, a collection of information subject to the requirements of the Paperwork Reduction Act of 1995, unless it displays a currently valid OMB control number. If you have any comments on this collection of information, please contact the Employer Services Team by email at employerservices@acf.hhs.gov.

Income Withholding for Support (IWO) Document Tracking ID ____________ Page 1 of 4

Employer/Income Withholder's Name: ______________________ Employer/Income Withholder's FEIN: ______________

Employee/Obligor's Name: ______________________________________ SSN: ______________

Case ID: ______________________ Order ID: ______________________

V. Remittance Information: (Completed by the Sender except for the "Return to Sender" check box.)

If the employee/obligor's principal place of employment is Alabama (State/Tribe), you must begin withholding no later than the first pay period that occurs 14 days after the date of service of the order/notice. Send payment within 7 business days of the pay date. If you cannot withhold the full amount of support for any or all orders for this employee/obligor, withhold _____ % of disposable income for all orders. If the employee/obligor's principal place of employment is not Alabama (State/Tribe), obtain withholding limitations, time requirements, the appropriate method to allocate among multiple child support cases/orders and any allowable employer fees from the jurisdiction of the employee/obligor's principal place of employment.

State-specific withholding limit information is available at www.acf.hhs.gov/css/resource/state-income-withholding-contacts-and-program-requirements. For tribe-specific contacts, payment addresses, and withholding limitations, please contact the tribe at www.acf.hhs.gov/sites/default/files/programs/css/tribal_agency_contacts_printable_pdf.pdf or www.bia.gov/tribalmap/DataDotGovSamples/tld_map.html.

You may not withhold more than the lesser of: 1) the amounts allowed by the Federal Consumer Credit Protection Act (CCPA) [15 USC §1673 (b)]; or 2) the amounts allowed by the law of the state of the employee/obligor's principal place of employment if the place of employment is in a state; or the tribal law of the employee/obligor's principal place of employment if the place of employment is under tribal jurisdiction. The CCPA is available at www.dol.gov/sites/dolgov/files/WHD/legacy/files/garn01.pdf. If the Order Information section does not indicate that the arrears are greater than 12 weeks, then the employer should calculate the CCPA limit using the lower percentage.

If there is more than one IWO against this employee/obligor and you are unable to fully honor all IWOs due to federal, state, or tribal withholding limits, you must honor all IWOs to the greatest extent possible, giving priority to current support before payment of any past-due support.

If the obligor is a nonemployee, obtain withholding limits from the **Supplemental Information** section in this IWO. This information is also available at www.acf.hhs.gov/css/resource/state-income-withholding-contacts-and-program-requirements.

Remit payment to ALABAMA CHILD SUPPORT PAYMENT CENTER (ACSPC) (SDU/Tribal Order Payee)
at P.O. BOX 244015, MONTGOMERY, AL 36124-4015 (SDU/Tribal Payee Address)

Include the Remittance ID with the payment and if necessary this locator code of the SDU/Tribal order payee ________ on the payment.

To set up electronic payments or to learn state requirements for checks, contact the State Disbursement Unit (SDU). Contacts and information are found at www.acf.hhs.gov/css/resource/sdu-eft-contacts-and-program-requirements.

☐ **Return to Sender (Completed by Employer/Income Withholder).** Payment must be directed to an SDU in accordance with sections 466(b)(5) and (6) of the Social Security Act or Tribal Payee (see Payments in Section VI). If payment is not directed to an SDU/Tribal Payee or this IWO is not regular on its face, you must check this box and return the IWO to the sender.

If Required by State or Tribal Law:
Signature of Judge/Issuing Official: ______________________
Print Name of Judge/Issuing Official: ______________________
Title of Judge/Issuing Official: ______________________
Date of Signature: ______________________

If the employee/obligor works in a state or for a tribe that is different from the state or tribe that issued this order, a copy of this IWO must be provided to the employee/obligor.

☐ If checked, the employer/income withholder must provide a copy of this form to the employee/obligor.

Employer/Income Withholder's Name: ______________________ Employer/Income Withholder's FEIN: ______________

Employee/Obligor's Name: ______________________________________ SSN: ______________

Case ID: ______________________________ Order ID: ______________________________

VI. Additional Information for Employers/Income Withholders: (Completed by the Sender)

Priority: Withholding for support has priority over any other legal process under State law against the same income (section 466(b)(7) of the Social Security Act). If a federal tax levy is in effect, please notify the sender.

Payments: You must send child support payments payable by income withholding to the appropriate State Disbursement Unit or to a tribal CSE agency within 7 business days, or fewer if required by state law, after the date the income would have been paid to the employee/obligor and include the date you withheld the support from his or her income. You may combine withheld amounts from more than one employee/obligor's income in a single payment as long as you separately identify each employee/obligor's portion of the payment. Child support payments may not be made through the federal Office of Child Support Enforcement (OCSE) Child Support Portal.

Lump Sum Payments: You may be required to notify a state or tribal CSE agency of upcoming lump sum payments to this employee/obligor such as bonuses, commissions, or severance pay. Contact the sender to determine if you are required to report and/or withhold lump sum payments. Employers/income withholders may use OCSE's Child Support Portal (ocsp.acf.hhs.gov/csp/) to provide information about employees who are eligible to receive lump sum payments and to provide contacts, addresses, and other information about their companies. Child support payments may not be made through the federal OCSE Child Support Portal.

Liability: If you have any doubts about the validity of this IWO, contact the sender. If you fail to withhold income from the employee/obligor's income as the IWO directs, you are liable for both the accumulated amount you should have withheld and any penalties set by state or tribal law/procedure. ______________________________

Section 30-3-69, Ala. Code 1975

Anti-discrimination: You are subject to a fine determined under state or tribal law for discharging an employee/obligor from employment, refusing to employ, or taking disciplinary action against an employee/obligor because of this IWO.

Section 30-3-70, Ala. Code 1975

Supplemental Information: ______________________________

Employer/Income Withholder's Name: ____________________ Employer/Income Withholder's FEIN: ________________

Employee/Obligor's Name: ____ SSN: ________________

Case ID: ______________________________ Order ID: ______________________________

VII. Notification of Employment Termination or Income Status: (Completed by the Employer/Income Withholder)

If this employee/obligor never worked for you or you are no longer withholding income for this employee/obligor, you must promptly notify the CSE agency and/or the sender by returning this form to the address listed in the **Contact Information** section below or using OCSE's Child Support Portal (ocsp.acf.hhs.gov/csp/). Please report the new employer or income withholder, if known.

☐ This person has never worked for this employer nor received periodic income.

☐ This person no longer works for this employer nor receives periodic income.

Please provide the following information for the employee/obligor:

Termination date: ______________________________ Last known telephone number: ________________

Last known address: ____

____

Final payment date to SDU/Tribal Payee: ________________ Final payment amount: ________________

New employer's or income withholder's name: ____

New employer's or income withholder's address: ____

____

VIII. Contact Information: (Completed by the Sender)

To Employer/Income Withholder: If you have questions, contact ______________________ (sender name) by telephone: ____________ , by fax: ____________ , by email or website: ______________________.

Send termination/income status notice and other correspondence to: ______________________________

____ (sender address).

To Employee/Obligor: If the employee/obligor has questions, contact ______________________ (sender name) by telephone: ____________, by fax: ____________, by email or website: ______________________.

IMPORTANT: The person completing this form is advised that the information may be shared with the employee/obligor.

Encryption Requirements:

When communicating this form through electronic transmission, precautions must be taken to ensure the security of the data. Child support agencies are encouraged to use the electronic applications provided by the federal Office of Child Support Enforcement. Other electronic means, such as encrypted attachments to emails, may be used if the encryption method is compliant with Federal Information Processing Standard (FIPS) Publication 140-2 (FIPS PUB 140-2).

INDEX

M

P

R

S

T

U

NOTES

Made in United States
Troutdale, OR
10/01/2026

55032815R00040